FINDING ERZILI

MARGARET MITCHELL ARMAND

FINDING ERZILI

ISBN-13: 978 -1492992325
ISBN-10: 1492992321

Credits

Artwork and Logo ©: Margaret Mitchell Armand
Vèvès Arts - Imani Collection by the author

KISKEYA PUBLISHING CO, LLC

We are loved!

Peace is a matter of the heart
La paix est une histoire de cœur
Tèt ansanm chita sou lanmou

Margaret Mitchell Armand, Ph.D.

4-26-14

FINDING ERZILI

Poetry is not only dream and vision; it is the skeleton architecture of our lives. It lays the foundations for a future of change, a bridge across our fears of what has never been before.

Audre Lorde

Écrite dans le sentiment de l'urgence, cette poésie en trois langues est le reflet immuable des émotions de Margaret Armand. Loin des exigences techniques, la poétesse nous confie les acquis d'une vie, ses pans de rêve, ses plaintives nostalgies. Elle nous livre un vécu où la fascination de l'irrémédiable ne peut supplanter l'espérance de rédemption.

Cette œuvre nous conforte dans la pensée que l'art ne peut être conçu qu'avec le souffle puissant de nos souffrances et de nos joies.

Merci pour ce partage Margaret, ta poésie nous parle jusqu'au fond de l'âme.

Dr. Marie Alice Théard
(IWA/ AICA)
Historienne de l'art

Strength comes from within; once you find it
everything else is possible.

Margaret Mitchell Armand

Happiness is, knowing where you are going
one minute at a time.

Margaret Mitchell Armand

Love is healing; apply liberally.

Margaret Mitchell Armand

CONTENTS

PREFACE

The philosophy of Realism in international relations outlined in the writing of Thucydides, Nicolo Machiavelli, Thomas Hobbes, and Henry Kissinger portrays human nature as nasty, brutish, and evil. Realpolitik dominates how people relate to each other nationally and globally dividing time, space, and people into the "haves" and the "have nots," the "in-group" and the "out group." The Realist practice operates in the realm of the cognitive side of the brain dividing nations, groups, and our very humanity. Gandhi, for example, said that in modern society the heart and mind are out of sync. The heart must reach the mind to create that synergy between the heart and the mind to focus on the truth and change the nature of the relationship between oppressed and oppressor. As Dr. Jessica Senehi stresses, the humanities expressed in storytelling, art, and poetry connects the heart of the person to what it truly means to be human. The humanities are a means of conflict intervention to make a difference to transform relationships and create real social change, realizing that socio-economic and political structures must be transformed too.

The humanities give voice to the disempowered to speak out, provide a system of indigenous knowledge, and connect people in the community. The creativity of the person is expressed in an inclusive fashion that represents the cultural identity and history of a community. The artist fosters love, equality, and empathy in her work. Everyone can participate and critically evaluate what is going on in their cultural milieu and political space. The humanities create the opportunity for the disempowered to forge a paradigm shift that creates possibilities for people to break out of the realist structural framework. Margaret makes the point in her poems that "the other reflects us, and if we deny the other, then we deny ourselves."

The humanities are influencing the transformationlists in the conflict resolution and peace-building field. Transformational conflict resolution theorists and practitioners work with the arts and humanities to promote reconciliation, forgiveness, interdependence, healing, empowerment, creativity, trust and relationship building, diversity, and justice in their work. They understand that macro structural as well as micro level changes have to be made if society is to become humanity centered.

Margaret Armand's honest and vibrant poetry clearly falls into this transformational tradition of theory and practice. She researched the role of identity, language, and conflict transformation in the *vodou* religion in Haiti. Margaret opened her heart to this field and broke the mold with her personal experience as a peace activist in her personal struggle to bring dignity to people that experience the same struggle in their native homeland. She has worked tirelessly as a peace activist for the poor, the disempowered, and the voiceless in South Florida, and Haiti. Margaret's poems astutely point out that, "we are all in the same bag, and we are human." This book of poetry illustrates how poetry is defined by cultures and its role in making change. Ms. Armand's first book of poetry gives the reader the essence of what it is that makes people human, and what is needed to build their self-esteem and self-efficacy. The book is a must read for teachers, artists, scholars, conflict resolution and peace practitioners, and community activists struggling to find their place in the middle of conflictual experiences imposed on them from society.

Sean Byrne, Ph.D., Director
Arthur V. Mauro Center for Peace and Justice
Saint Paul's College
University of Manitoba

INTRODUCTION

My poetry is a reflection of the journey of my soul in particular time and space that brings magic to my life. It is often thought-provoking as it interrogates, shares, brings into perspective, writes back, questions, talkback, defends, speaks out, brings close, teaches, shows gratitude, understands, nurtures, remembers, dreams, honors, gives hope, cherishes and above all Heal and LOVE. It is a medium through which the creative energies of ancestral legacies flow in their relentlessness to provide immense satisfaction while transforming what I feel to a clearly defined outcome. The poems coalesce with the sacred arts of the *Vèvè* that offer the testimony of spiritual powers.

The *Vèvè* art design on the cover of the book is my own artistic expression that merges art and poetry. It is *"Erzili,"* the Lwa of love; she stands as the reminder that the heart's ancestral memory guides us and transforms the obstacles to personal peace. It is a statement of my freedom, an act of faith rooted in tradition. It is a celebration of our common ground to create harmony.

In this poetry book, Finding Erzili, the Lwa of love, I have added the love poems of my father William Francois Mitchell to my mother Anne-Marie Solages, nascent to their love for each other. I am honoring the lessons and love they share with me.

The poems in this book are in English, French, Haitian Kreyòl, and Spanish. These poems are expressed in languages that I have learned.

LEGBA GRANCHIMEN

Papa Legba ouvè baryè pou mwen
lè m a tounen m a remèsye lwa yo.
Annou mache papa Legba annou mache.
Annou mache papa Legba annou mache
pou n ale wè sa ki genyen nan kay la.
Annou mache vye kanyan annou mache
pou nou ale wè ki sa k ap kòmande.

Papa Legba open the gate for me.
I will be so thankful.
Let's go papa Legba, let's go old man,
show me the way.

LEGBA GRANCHIMEN

MEETING OF SOULS

Our path crossed many times
Yet it was not time
Until our eyes met again
Our hands grasped this chance
To touch each other

I heard your soul
Talk to mine
Asking for us
To reach again
To each other

That day came
You heard my song
You liked the word
You felt the love
Saw your life there

Love peace and kindness
Is what got us here

MAMAN

I am this child growing inside you
Telling you how much I need you
Maman
I feel your love
Hear your words
You feed me
Warm me
Take me
Everywhere you go
I feel so safe
In your warm body
Feeling your tender soul
Waiting for me
Maman
I love you so
Will you ever know
That I have chosen you
To help me this way
So I can become
The best I can be
For you
Maman
I love you

MY SISTER ROSIE

From the torrent of my life
My soul feels your presence
You are in my blood
Mine runs through yours
I search for your face
I know you are there
I breathe your existence
Is it our fate to be separated
An explosion of light
A fireworks of love
Reunited at last

IMANI, MY GRAND DAUGHTER

Welcome to my life
For the joy you bring
The calmness of your soul
The passion in your eyes
The tenderness of your touch
The kindness in your heart
I have been waiting for you
What took you so long
Too much to do
Too many lessons to learn
You are ready now
So am I

ANAKAONA, MA PETITE FLEUR D'OR

Tu inspires l'amour et la paix
À tout ce qui t'entoure
Ta beauté séduisante
Reflète la candeur de ton âme
Que nos Lwas te protègent
Et guident tes pas
Que tes chemins soient remplis
D'amour et de sagesse
Que ta vie soit longue
Heureuse et fructueuse
Tu es ma petite fleur d'or
Anakaona

AKINLE

Akinle, my courageous grandson
We have met before
Life got us back here again
It is this infinite place
Facing new challenges
That would be in our way
To teach, Love and share
For you, for me and all of us
I love you

FOR ASHOKA

I am ready for your love
Do I wait like the dove
In an iron cage
With no hope of freedom

I am ready for your love
Will you come one day
And open my heart
To heal those wounds

I am ready for love
Do not wait too long
Life is going away
Every day

I am ready for your love
Still waiting patiently
Hoping to see you
One day

I am ready for your love
Will you ever show your face
To bring back to my life
All that was loss in vain
You are here today
I love you I say

LOULOUCE
(My first son passing in spirit)

Is it you I hear in the silence of the night
Is it you the light that blinks in the starry night
The wings of the butterfly brush the yellow hibiscus
Is it you
The perfume in my room is of gardenia
Is it you
I lose my ring and suddenly it appears
Is it you
Laying in my bed I feel your embrace
I know it is you
I miss you

FINDING ERZILI

Erzili Goddess of Love

ERZILI VÈVÈ

FINDING ERZILI

Erzili you have always been there
In the darkness of the night
To give strength to my soul
To give light to my thoughts
My body trembles from the pain of life
You wake me and I feel your love
You travel from far yet you are near

Africa, Ayiti, Ginen!

I am here you are there
We are both here and there
To reclaim what is lost
I scream your name
I feel your power
Erzili mother of us all

ÈZILI FANM LANMOU

Ou toujou mache ak mwen
Lè la vi ap maspinen m
Ou mete chalè nan kè m
Ou pote limyè nan wout mwen
Lè doulè lanmou
Ap sakaje m
Ou montre m sa ki lanmou
Se lanmou ki ban m fòs
Se lanmou ki ban m jarèt
Ou tout kote
Èzili fanm lanmou
Nan Lafrik
Ayiti nan Ginen
Ou bannou chimen lakay
Chimen ou se lanmou
Pouvwa ou se lanmou
Pouvwa pa m se lanmou
Ou se mwen m se ou
Èzili ou se manman noutout

LANMOU SE PLEZI M

Lanmou se plezi m lè Imani tonbe ri
Lanmou se plezi m lè Kluzo kouri jwenn mwen
Ak zorèy li pandye
Lanmou se plezi m lè Michou mache bwodè
Lè mwen ba li manje
Lanmou se plezi m lè Loulouce fè yon bwi
Pou m vire gade
Lanmou se plezi m lè Alain byen mennen
Li gen kè kontan
Lanmou se plezi m lè Babette di m
Ou se yon bon manman
Lanmou se plezi m lè Akinle souri
Lanmou se plezi m ki fè m santi m fanm
Lanmou se plezi ki ban m kè kontan
Se lanmou ki ban m lavi
Se lanmou ki ban m jarèt
Lanmou dwe nan lavi nou tout

LOVE IS KNOCKING AT MY DOOR

Love is knocking at my door
Once more ready to lay my naked soul
For the sacrifice of the gods
Furnace burning my body
Temple of Lwa
Willing to deliver
This incessant fury
Longing to be awaken
Gasping pushing
Thrilling to breathe the ecstasy
Through the temple
For love

DANCE IN ECSTASY

Dance to the sound of music
It does not matter the place
Barefoot and free
It could be the banjo
Let's dance the tango
Or the drum beating for the gathering
While the guitar is ready to
Serenade my heart
Is the flute much better languorously
Calling out the mermaid
From the deep ocean
The trumpet will do, so will the piano
But the saxophone will shake me up
And make my body move
Dance with the flow of life
The happiness of being
Just here at this point in time

CATCH ME IF YOU CAN

Catch me in the running
From my sorrow
Catch the flowers I am holding
Follow the trail of my perfume
In the mist of the green meadow
Surrender your love to my being
I am clinging to the innocence of loving
Yet afraid of this slippery road

Laughing at the irony of our meeting
Seeing in your deep dark eyes
The passion for giving
Waiting for me
To stop running
I am standing now on solid ground
Waiting for the homecoming

WANGA NÈGÈS

Mwen se yon Wanga Nègès
Ki fèt nan solèy
Lalin se manman mwen
Lavi se fanmi mwen
Yo voye m sou latè
Pou mwen pote limyè
Mwen souse nan tout flè
M jwenn sekrè
M abiye wouj e ble
Se koulè drapo mwen
Lò ak lajan kouvri zèl mwen
Nan fènwa yo pa wè m
M klere nan limyè
M pote maji
Chans ak bonè
Lanmou anba zèl mwen
Pou tout moun sou latè

THE HUMMINGBIRD

I am a hummingbird
Born in the sun
All my friends are on earth
I am sent this way
To bring joy to the world
I suck all the flowers
I know their secrets
I escape the darkness
Carry light where I go
Bright reds and deep blues
Gold and silver are mine
Rushing from one spot to another
I capture the celestial magic
To bring luck happiness
Lots of love on my wings
To spread it everywhere

FOR YOU I STAY

I am a woman
I feel the pain
A child is gone
A love lost
I dream of the day
When I would go away
But what would I do
If I stayed for you
You are coming my way
To brighten my days

FINDING ERZILI

OGOU

The Lwa of courage; the defender of social justice.

OGOU VÈVÈ

OGOU

Horseman of the night
Companion of the day
Brandishing your sword
Looking for your children
We are hurt
We are drowned
We are murdered
We suffer silently
We have traveled to faraway places
We have been fooled
But you Ogou slowly
You find us one by one
You take our hand
And show us the path
To victory

OGOU

Chevalier de la nuit
Compagnon du jour
L'épée à la main
Tu vas clopin-clopant
Cherchant tes enfants
Nous avons faim
Nous avons soif
On nous blesse
On nous tue
On nous noie
Nous souffrons en silence
Nous courons vers d'autres horizons
Nous sommes dupes
Mais toi
Ogou
Tout doucement
Tu nous trouves un à un
Nous prends par la main
Nous ramènent
À la maison

REVOLUTION

Slavery, Colonization, MisEducation
This is not Haiti's independence
Two hundred years of locked doors
Surviving only to fight or to kill each other
Our ancestor's tears rush down the ocean
Like brown waters reaping through our mountains
Like the back of enslaved Africans
Our forefathers
Young men standing in street corners
Eyes blood shut from hunger
Young children with their belly protruding
Women watching hopelessly their lives go by
Drums beating all nights
Constant reminder of that place called Africa.
How did we get here from there?
Have we forgotten?
Let us stand again and claim our Independence
To open wide those doors slammed in our faces!!!

LET OUR CONSCIENCE SPEAK

For the trees being cut
The charcoal we are buying
For the vote we are not casting
For the taxes we are not paying
For watching the thieves take over
Haiti and selling
It piece by piece
While our friends are part of the doing
We are saying nothing
For letting the sick in this filth
For the schools not built
Some Christian NGOs buy Haitian souls
With second hand clothes and a few cans of goods
Getting the tax rebate in their own country
While *Vodou* is persecuted
Our tradition is not respected
We are selling the future of our children
Let's our conscience speak
Let it scream
Enough, enough, enough!

DRAPO PEYI MWEN

Desalin chire w
Katrin Flon koud ou
Ble e wouj ou te ye
Nwa e wouj ou tounen
Yo fann ou nan mitan

Ou kanpe yon bo wouj
Lòtbò ou tounen ble
Yo vire ou chita
Wouj anba ble anwo

Kounye a li ta dwe rete
Pwoblèm la se pa ou
Se noumenm ki pa sèten

Ni konnen kiyès nou ye
Lè jou sa a va rive
N a sispann sakaje w
Ou toujou rete drapo nou

BLOODLINES

Soft black hair around my face
Like the night of an Irish landscape
Flowing like the wind of France
In a cool spring day
Shining like olive oil
From the hills of Spain
I search the unknown
Like a Corsican ship in the Caribbean Sea
Fleeting toward Haiti
I claim to be the daughter of the African queen
Of the dynasty of Dahomey
Bloodlines of Lwas clinging
To my body and claiming my soul
For the message of forgiveness and peace

For the Arawaks that were murdered
In my homeland of Haiti
Where Africans from Dahomey Congo Nago
Wangol Niger Senegal Ethiopia…
Endured the horror of slavery
Let's tell their story and bring forth their courage
Honoring the home where we all began
Africa the birthplace of our humanity

NATIVE LAND

Chilling on the white sand on the island of Haiti
Caressed by the froth
Of the emerald sea of the Caribbean
Warmed by the hands of the hot sun of my country
Clouds color of ocean froth
Dance to the music of yellow birds
Melodies that rekindle sweet memories
Of my wild youth
A red hibiscus flower in full bloom
Moves its yellow pistil close to my ear
Softly murmurs
And speaks ever so gently
Come back to your home
Beautiful lady
We are all ready to rebuild
The magic island Haiti

FINDING ERZILI

AGAOU

Agaou is the Lwa who rules over thunder, rain, lightning, wind, storm and earthquake.

AGAOU VÈVÈ

VODOU LAKAY MWEN

Mwen chita nan yon kwen
M ap koute m ap gade
Tou sa yo di sou ou
Kout lang
Ki ta dwe fè m wont
Yon loray kale
Agaou gwonde
M leve kanpe
Vodou peyi mwen
Mwen konnen ou se fòs mwen
E yo konnen sa tou

KI MESAJ OU POTE ?

Ki mesaj ou pote
Si se tripotay
M pa bezwen konnen
Si se dezinyon, manti ak kout lang
Kanpe lwen m
Mwen pa tande
Mwen gen anpil bagay serye pou m okipe
Se sèlman men nan lamen n a rive

Ki mesaj ou pote
Si se lanmou wap bay
La pè ak linyon
Pataj konesans
Rekonsilyasyon
M a chita tande w

ZANMI MWEN

Lè ou gen yon zanmi
Ke li se gason ke I se fanm
Dyakout ou chaje ak lanmou
Lè yo malad ou kanpe
Lè yo bezwen èd ou la
Lè yo gen lapenn ou konsole yo
Lè yo pale sa yo pa konnen
Ou rele anmwe ou toujou pare
Pou limen limyè verite
Moun ki pa konnen ki moun ou ye
Pito gade ou sou kote

Yo pale sa yo pa wè
Se pa anyen yo genyen
Yo ta renmen konnen
Ki jan djakout ou fè plen
Mwen ki zanmi ou fouye
Nan djakout kè ou pote
Ou toujou pare pou separe
Sa ou genyen
Sekrè ou se libète

VOICES – *SILENCE OF HOPE*

Sounds of misunderstood words
Sounds of endless pains
Sounds of unknown languages
Sounds that divide humanity
Sounds that penetrate my soul
Tearing my hopes shredding my dreams
In thousand pieces
Then the silence comes
Silence to calm my body
Feelings of love to heal my soul
Wrapping my spirit with soft memories
Preparing me for new melody

I AM FREAKING OUT

Shotguns through my door
Children scream
Hang on to me
Screams of fear
Call for help
Green hard hats
Dirty uniforms
Bullets streak through the wall
Lights out
Phone cords cut
Get your butt out there
Neighbors one by one
Turn lights on
Scared gunmen run away
In the dark starless night
I am freaking out
Not giving up the fight

FINDING ERZILI

LOKO ATISOU is the Lwa that passes on the knowledge during the initiation process in the Vodou religion. This knowledge is symbolized by the sacred Ason (below) that serves as tool to communicate to the
Lwas of the ancestors.

Loko Atisou symbolizes the guardian of Haiti's traditional Vodou religion.

The vèvè at the right upper corner represents the symbol of Loko Atisou.

LOKO ATISOU VÈVÈ

GET ON GOING

Clothes that do no longer fit
Thoughts controlling your mind
Twisting tangling dangling
Keeping you from flying
Like a bird in the sky
Holding a twig
That will drop on the ground
As soon as he tries to sing
Discard the trapping
The crooked believing
Let go of that useless twig
The wind of freedom
Will take you to a horizon
Of sharing giving caring
Singing and living

LAMAYÒT

Lamayòt m pa pè ou se moun ou ye
You do not scare me Lamayòt
With your colorful costumes of Mardi Gras
Powdered face
Box full of tricks
I know who you are
Lamayòt
You are my friend
Ou se zanmi mwen
Fòk ou degize
Nan madigra

Pour m'approcher et me parler
Me faire jouir de mon enfance
Derrière un masque

That makes me laugh
And cry at the same time

Thanks Lamayòt

AYITI

Se yon bon peyi zansèt nou ban nou
Desandan Endyen Afriken Franse Panyòl ak zòt
Nou se Ayisyen
Nap soufri yon doulè andedan zantray nou
Nou tout Ayisyen
Nou se Ayisyen
Moun pòv moun rich
N ap sekle n ap plante
Moun deyò moun andedan
Komèsan machann pwofesè
Filozòf doktè travayè mandyan timoun lari
Nou se Ayisyen
Jistis Egalite Rekonsilyasyon
Se sa nou bezwen
Pou nou ka santi
Tout bon nou se Ayisyen

GREASY POLE / MASWUIFE

Men climb the greasy pole
On the park in Port-au-Prince
People cheering watching eyes
Jumping from excitement
Supporting
Helping with encouraging
Sounds and words
Families friends the *fresco* seller
The peanut and *tito* merchant
Bystanders in unison

Sun scorching black strong bodies
Clothes soaked with grease and sweat
Mixed with ashes used for climbing

Women are intrigued
All that fuss
We women are climbing
Every day the greasy pole of life

PAYS NATAL

Me prélassant sur un sable gris
Sous le soleil chaud d'Haïti
Des oiseaux bleus aux becs roux
Sifflotent les chansons de mon pays
Des nuages blancs dans un ciel bleu
Dansent leurs mélodies
Bercée par la cadence des vagues
Un rêve fou me poursuit
Je revis les moments heureux
Que j'ai connus
Une voix douce me dit
Belle femme d'Haïti
Reste dans ton pays
À rebâtir ta patrie
Haïti chérie

RECLAIMING

Lonely and feeling in the dump
Got me in reclaiming
Am I the nothingness
That they are claiming
Not so
They are in the darkness
They have created
But not for me
I know the true meaning
Of their ways of doing
The light shines in me
It validates the feeling
Of being part of that
Divine force of being human

GRANBWA

Granbwa is the Lwa of the forest, the great healer;
he also symbolizes the healing power of love.

GRANBWA VÈVÈ

PRAYER OF GRIEF AND JOY

Grieving for my son,
I hear God's voice

> *I sent you a child of mine for a little time*
> *For you to love while he lives*
> *And remember when he is in spirit*
> *You took such good care of him*
> *and now I need him home*
> *I wanted this child to learn lessons to use*
> *when he returns.*
> *I searched throughout the whole wide world*
> *for a teacher's true*
> *and I have chosen you.*
> *The labor is not vain and now he is safely home.*
> *We both are watching over you.*

Dear God, for the happiness I have known with him,
I say

> *I will forever grateful be.*
> *Thy will be done.*

May we find happiness in the memories that are never for-
gotten!

THE ROSE

Did you know that I compare you to a kiss from a rose?
That I see your beauty and Love as a thing to be feared
And not embraced
That to admire that beauty from afar in frustration
Is merely an attempt to keep my blood from escaping
The comfort and protection of my veins
How could you when I act as if you are not there
Every time I pass you
So I stand and watch you blossom into that
Most coveted flower knowing that I need only to pick you
To fully enjoy what you have shown me
Seemingly paralyzed by Histories lessons
And knowing that a rose is not a rose without the thorns

Lucien Georges Armand, My son
9/26/1971 - 5/28/1998

TOGETHER

We are all in this together
We want the same
Love Peace
For our brothers and sisters
A place to be and feel that connection
Life takes us everywhere
Together we will be
This place must be
For us to be
Work to be done
To make it so
Love to share
With each other
And all the others

DREAMING

Feelings that give meaning to life
Hoping for that dream to come
Glimpsing how that day will be
Fearing never to see
That place to be
Dreading never to feel
That bliss
Out of this fear
I am strong
I am waiting to be home again

THE WALL

There is a wall around you
A place created only by you
It takes a toll to be in it
You built it to feel safe
Thinking that it would help
To protect you from the unknown
It prevents you from breathing
The clean air that comes in
You stay in it and you will die
Open you will feel free
Then you will know
Why you did it
And find your place out of it

ALORS LA VIE ME DIT

Écoute la musique de ton âme
Regarde avec les yeux d'un aveugle
Respire le parfum de ton cœur
Alors tu découvriras
Que tu peux tendre la main à ton frère
Brise les chaines des lois
Qui sont faites par des humains
Prends ton honneur par la main
Pour ceux qui te tendent leur cœur
Pour aller vers le chemin
Qui nous conduit tous dans ce lieu
Où nous pourrons ensemble
Vivre dans un monde
Où sans parole nous saurons
Ce que c'est vraiment partager

LE TEMPS PASSE

Mon âme seule entend ta voix
Perdue dans un milieu inconnu de moi
Ma prière s'élève dans les cieux
Pour te dire combien de feux
J'ai traversé pour t'aider
Je porte encore une lourde pierre
Tout au fond de mon cœur
Ta vie encore continue
Je la porte à main nue
Pour les jours heureux connus
Ton visage si beau et tendre
Ton cœur rempli de joie
Tes éclats de rire contagieux
Qui me donnent du courage
Ces souvenirs de bonheur
Me donne encore du courage
Je t'aime et je prie pour nous
Je te réclame souvent auprès de moi
Dans la tristesse de mes nuits
Et de mes jours éprouvés
Je m'assombrie des milliers de fois
Mais garde avec moi l'espoir
D'être réunie un jour avec toi

PEACE

Is it possible
In this confused world
Where chaos reigns
Not knowing whom to believe
Who to really trust
How can it be peace if I stay silent
Watching and hoping for things to change
I want peace
Peace for all the children
And the children to be
Yes for all the children
I cannot teach peace
I can only show the path
For each act of peace is
A child saved
A world changed

LA PAIX

Est-il possible
Dans ce monde confus
Où le chaos règne
Ne sachant qui croire
À qui faire vraiment confiance
Comment cela peut être la paix si je reste silencieuse
Observant et espérant que les choses changeront
Je veux la paix
La paix pour tous les enfants
Et les enfants à venir
Oui pour tous les enfants
Je ne peux pas enseigner la paix
Je peux seulement montrer le chemin
Car, chaque acte de paix est
Un enfant sauvé
Un monde changé

LA PAZ

Es posible
En este mundo desesperado
Sin confianza por nadie

No es La Paz si yo me quedo sin hablar
Y sin hacer nada para ayudar
Esperando que las cosas cambian
Yo quiero La Paz
Para todos los niños
Y los niños del futuro
Yo no puedo enseñar La Paz
Yo puedo solamente mostrar el camino
Cada acción de Paz
Es una lección de Paz
Un niño salvado y un mundo mejor

Yo no puedo mantener mi silencio
Ni quedarme sin hacer nada
Para ayudar a los niños

MI PAÍS

Tú estás bonita
Pero desnuda como una vieja
Sin respeto por nada
Te llama mi país
Yo te quiero
Pero estoy lejos de ti
Muchas veces yo quiero
Ir a protegerte
Pero a nadie le importa
Al verte así
Espero que un día
Tengas una sonrisa
Que me digas
Yo espero verte aquí
No es que falta
Amor y sinceridad
Es que tu cara
Parece a una carta
De recuerdos
De angustia
Hay que cambiar
El destino
Y abrir la puerta
Para que el amor
Llena la isla de perla

INFINITE LOVE

Smell of jasmine nourishing the space
Saffron painted bodies moving resolutely
Candles floating on the Ganges River
Spirit awakening with the sunrise
Asserting eternity
Light Light Light
Bursting with memories
Chanting digging and evoking
Sitting on a floating canoe
Music dances healing
Inhaling sandalwood smoke
Yellow gold orange marigolds
Gliding toward
Shiva's temple
A déjà vu
Reclaiming an eternal moment
Witness a union of souls
An eternal love

À UN HAITIEN NOYÉ - DÉSESPOIR

Décidé à chercher un avenir meilleur
Encouragé par les possibilités d'ailleurs
Survivant à peine dans ta patrie
Exaspéré par la futilité de ta vie
Sentant de la faim la morsure continue
Partant sur le canot vermoulu
Osant affronter la pleine mer
Inanimé et froid tu es devenu
Reposes en paix frère de ma terre

Dr. Lucien Armand

FINDING ERZILI

MÈT KAFOU
Master of the Crossroads

MÈT KAFOU VÈVÈ

Master of the Crossroads

MY YOUTH; MEMORABLE MOMENTS!

Margaret Mitchell Armand 3 years old

CARREFOUR-FEUILLE

As tall as a 2 feet wall
I am standing on my toes to look up high
The luminous sun setting to sleep in the ocean
Behind the hill facing my home
Planting a rose garden in a field of weeds
While chickens are coming to feed
I wait patiently to smell the first rosebud
Holding firmly my grandmother's hand
Listen to the drops of waterfall
Dripping from the shimmering hole
Of the cave
Nested deep in the lush mountain
Behind our home
God and Lwas inhabit this cave
For the water that grants us life
Haitian women and children in line
Fill their white enamel buckets
On their way down the hills of Carrefour-Feuille
God lives there I said
My father smiles lovingly at me in approval
Then hold me tight
My grandma and my dad
Have moved on as ancestors
Innocent children's dead bodies are buried
Under the post-earthquake rubbles
Of my childhood home
May their spirits rest in peace
I am here to pick up the pieces
And find a way to reach others.

CARREFOUR-FEUILLE

Pas plus haute qu'un mur de 60 centimètres
Je me hisse sur la pointe des pieds pour voir en haut
Le soleil lumineux près à s'endormir dans la mer
Derrière la montagne face à ma maison
Un jardin de roses fleurit dans un chant d'herbes
Alors que les poules viennent y becqueter
J'ai patiemment attendu l'odeur du premier bouton
Tenant fermement la main de ma grand'mère
Écoutant les gouttes d'eau
Dégouliner à travers le trou scintillant
De la cave
Profondément nichée dans la montagne verdoyante
Derrière ma maison
Dieu et esprits habitent la cave
Avec l'eau qui nous donne la vie
Femmes et enfants haïtiens en ligne
Remplissent leurs seaux en émail blanc
En descendant les collines de Carrefour-Feuille
Dieu habite là je dis
Mon père m'approuve avec un sourire d'amour
Puis me serre bien fort
Ma grand'mère et mon père
Sont devenus des ancêtres
Corps morts d'enfants innocents sont engloutis
Par le tremblement de terre sous les ruines
De ma maison d'enfance
Que leurs esprits reposent en paix
C'est à moi qu'il revient de ramasser les morceaux
Et de trouver la voie qui conduit aux autres

KAFOU-FÈY

Pa pi wo pase yon mi de pye wotè
Sou pwent pye m mwen ise pou gade enwo
Solèy klere a kap pare pou rantre dòmi nan lanmè
Dèyè mòn nan anfas lakay mwen
Yon jaden woz ap fleri nan raje
Alòske poul yo ap vin chèche manje
Map tann ak pasyans odè yon premye bouton wòz
Men m kenbe men grann mwen fè m
Lè m ap koute dlo goutagout
Tonbe nan twou latè
Kav la
Ki pran nich li pami bèl vèdi nan mòn lan
Dèyè lakay mwen
Bondye ak lespri yo pran rasin nan kav la
Poutèt dlo ban nou lavi
Fanm ak timoun ayisyen kanpe an liy
Pou yo ranpli bokit emaye blan yo
Lè y ap desann mòn Kafou-Fèy
Bondye rete la mwen di
Papa m apwouve m ak yon souri damou
Epi li kenbe m byen sere
Grann mwen ak papa m
Pase nan milye zansèt yo
Tranblemanntè a anglouti
Kadav timoun inosan anba debri
Kay kote m grandi
Nou swete trankilite pou lespri yo
Mwen la pou mwen ranmase moso yo
Epi chèche mwayen pou jwenn lezòt

4TH OF JULY

It was the 4th of July 1969
In a small apartment in New York
Aunt Maud, aunt *Tètè* and the uncles and cousins
My mother strong as usual ready to start her new life
My father guarding privately the deep
Nostalgia of homeland
My younger brothers were playing
With the cousins

Grandma, *Manman Nennenn*, my godmother
Looked tenderly at me
Sitting on the edge of my small cot
I hold a book full of English words

In a brisk voice, she called her husband
Papa Roger, to read her the daily news as he did
in Haiti. She loved the news, the *teledyòl*

We knew little English then, the newspaper read
4th of July celebration
She turned to me and said in Haitian Kreyòl
Maggy, are you doing your homework;
This holiday is not yours?

We children knew
To respect and obey her.
Yes, Manman Nennenn I answered
I am learning English.
Later that day, we all sat around a
Small table for the family meal
Poul an sòs, diri kole ak pwa, national meal of Haiti.
We ate so much to fill the hole of sadness
The feeling of not belonging
In the bed that night,
I wet my pillow with my tears
And realized for the first time
That my life had changed forever.
January 1st, 1804 and July 4th
I learned to walk between two worlds
And find my place in it

AYIBOBO

Ayibobo for Anakaona, Taíno Queen
Ayibobo for the independence of Haiti in 1804
Ayibobo for Defilé
Ayibobo for Manbo Marie-Jeanne at la Crète à Pierrot
Ayibobo for Manbo Cecile
Ayibobo for Hougan Boukman at Bwa Kayiman
Ayibobo for Hougan Verneus Pierre-Paul
At La Gosseline, Jacmel
Ayibobo for Manbo Vernelie at Grand-Goâve
Ayibobo for Adelina in Port-au-Prince
Ayibobo for Hougan Papa Klo
Ayibobo for all the ancestors
Known and unknown...
They paved the way for us today

Je partage avec vous les poèmes d'amour de mon père William François Mitchell dédiés à ma mère Anne-Marie Solages. Ils se sont mariés le 22 décembre 1949.

FINDING ERZILI

De papa à maman
Love poems from my father to my mother

William François Mitchell et Anne-Marie Solages
marries à Port-au-Prince, Haïti le 22 décembre 1949

L'INTUITION DE MON ÂME

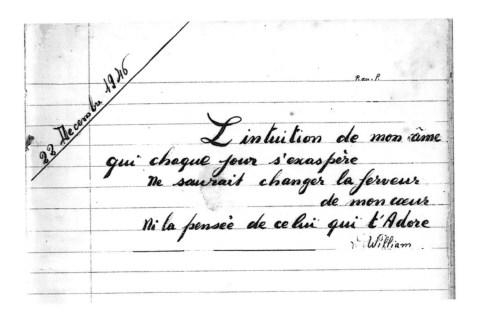

SOIR DE FÉVRIER

Port-au-Prince, Haïti 1945

Te souviens-tu du soir ?
Du soir ou nos regards
Tendrement vivifiés
Sous les verts lataniers
Ont su trouver en nous
Cet adoré Joujou
Pourtant nous étions là
Chassant tous les appâts
Qui veulent en ce bonheur
Me ravir ton doux cœur
Et tu me disais tout bas
D'une voix pleine d'émoi
« Je t'aime mon amour
Encore plus que le jour »
Alors dépossédé
J'appelle l'hyménée
Dilemme en vérité
De cueillir un baiser
Une passion m'excite
En mon âme subsiste
Car cet amour muet
Me rendait très inquiet
J'ai dû l'ensevelir
Pour chasser le désir
Je peux le dire : pour moi
Tu étais Nausicaa
Et quand ce souvenir
En mon cœur respire
Et quand nos passions enfouies
Se sont évanouies
Alors que je comprends
Demain ! À tout instant
Ce que c'est qu'aimer
              Avec Réalité
                    À toi mon indissoluble amour

SOIR DE FÉVRIER - 1945

Soir de Février. 1945
P. au. P.

Te souviens tu du soir ?
Du soir où nos regards,
Tendrement vivifiés
Sous les verts lataniers
Ont su trouver en nous
Cet adoré Jou Jou.
Pourtant nous étions là
Chassant tous les appâts
Qui veulent en ce bonheur
Me ravir ton doux cœur
Et tu me disais tout bas
D'une voix plein d'émoi:
« Je t'aime mon amour
Encore plus que le jour ».
Alors dépossédé
J'appelle l'hyménée
Dilemme en verité
De cueillir un baiser.
Une passion m'excite
En mon âme subsiste
Car cet amour muet
Me rendait très inquiet.
J'ai dû l'ensevelir.

Pour chasser le désir
Je peux le dire : pour moi
Tu étais Nausicaa.
Et quand ce souvenir
En mon cœur respire,
Quand nos passions enfouies
Se sont évanouies
Alors que je comprends
Demain ! à tout instant
Ce que c'est qu'aimer
    Avec Réalité
        A toi mon indissoluble Amour
          William

WILLIAM

CARNAVAL ACROSTICHE – MARS 1945

mars 1945

P. au. P.

Carnaval emblème de mon premier amour. Pour
  quoi es tu revenu !.
Apportes - tu des rêves superflus
Reviens - tu avec tes doux souvenirs
Nes - tu pas la source d'un bel avenir
Aujourd'hui ! demain ! et à tout instant
Veux - être le messager d'un amant
Ah carnaval puisque tu réponds Oui !
Les souvenirs, dans mon cœur pour tou-
  jours, seront enfouis.

William

FIFIE ACROSTICHE - MARS 1945

Acrostiche

Mars 1945

P. au. P.

Fuir un si grand amour. C'est mourir
Ignorer ce bonheur c'est souffrir.
Fructifions nous de zèle, de tendresse
Introuvable et suprème déesse
En toi règne l'amour pur et fatal
Envré, né un soir de Carnaval

mars 1945

P. au. P.

PRÉCAUTION

Port-au-Prince, Haïti - Mars 1945

Je ne connais d'autre cœur
Si ce n'est que le tien
Tu es aussi pour moi
Ce que je suis pour toi
Je t'aime pensez-y-bien
Toujours la jalousie, la rancœur
Passionnément tu m'affoles
Chérie ! Ne sois pas frivole
Repousse ma petite, mon amour
Ces adversaires, ces troubadours
Qui enivrés de passions
Son sujet aux moindres actions

William

30 Avril 1945 - Port-au-Prince, Haïti

Je t'assure William, rien au monde ne pourra briser le lien qui existe entre nous. Car mon amour est sincère. Je crois en toi et quand je te parle je ne dis que la vérité.

> Je ne ferai rien pour te déplaire
> Je te laisse : à bientôt
> Ta bien-aimée

Anne-Marie Solages

TON MOUCHOIR

Anse d'Hainault, Haïti, juillet 1946

Ce petit carré blanc baigné de ton parfum
Souvenir de tes doigts délicatement bruns
Ce mouchoir adoré que ce soir je contemple
Est comme un univers où nous sommes ensemble
Il se cache pour moi sous la splendeur du blanc
Ton souriant visage et l'éclat de tes yeux
Tout bas j'entends ta voix me dire ta détresse
La souffrance.......
Qui ronge ta jeunesse
Et tout ce que j'entends et tout ce que je vois
Sous ce mouchoir soyeux c'est mon amour pour toi
C'est un chant langoureux c'est un vibrant poème
C'est tout ce qui dans toi fait le bébé que j'aime
Voilà pourquoi m'amour je porte sur mon cœur
Le splendide cadeau beau fruit de ta ferveur
Je retrouve ta grâce et le blanc de ton rêve
Un impossible rêve englouti dans une grève
De ce carré tout blanc baigné de ton parfum
Souvenir de tes doigts délicatement bruns
Je respire l'amour et la senteur exquise
Et je m'endors grisé, caressé par la brise

William

MA DESTINÉE FIFIE

Port-au-Prince, Haïti ce 21 décembre 1946

Oui ! Quand tout me parait
Souvent sans lendemain
Quand pour moi tout est vain
Même les plus doux attraits
Une ombre visionnaire
Fait revivre en mon être
Une voix qui m'est chère
Si douce à reconnaitre
Cette voix c'est ta voix
Cette ombre c'est ton ombre
C'est toi cette belle et rare fleur
Je t'aime chérie
Je t'aime à en mourir
Je te demande enfin
Pourquoi me prives-tu
De ton doux parfum rare
À ma respiration de tes douces lèvres
D'où je recueillerai dans un long baiser
La sève nourricière de notre naissant amour
Pour me rendre heureux
Pour mieux me consoler
À me comprendre chercher
Tels en sont tous mes vœux

William

SÉNAT

On l'appelait « Sénat », Je n'ai jamais connu son nom de famille. Parfois ma tante prenait une voix théâtrale et lançait un retentissant « Sénateur » ! On le voyait arriver de sa démarche spéciale, ses larges pieds nus foulant le sol, habillé de gros bleu, son éternel panama sur la tête. Je me revois toute petite, débarquant du camion de « Déjuste ». Sénat et un de mes oncles étaient là, accompagnés de chevaux et de « bourriques », pour nous conduire à Gaspard, pays de mes ancêtres, à Fond-des-Blancs. Je me souviens des cris de joie, des embrassades. Maman, qui à Port-au-Prince passait pour une femme sévère et réservée, devenait soudain resplendissante, et ses beaux yeux bleus brillaient de bonheur ! – Elle me confiait à Sénat « *Men pitit ou* ». Il me disait avec beaucoup d'émotion dans la voix :
« *Mayou pitit mwen* ! » (Mayou, mon enfant). Sa main rugueuse prenait la mienne, et c'était le début de mes vacances !

Etant la petite dernière, je restais surtout dans la cour, à moins que mes grandes sœurs ne me fassent la faveur de me prendre avec elles. Mais, des années plus tard, plusieurs d'entre elles étaient déjà mariées. Mona, de quatre ans mon ainée, préférant aller à Port-de-Paix avec son amie Marie Louise, je me suis retrouvée seule avec maman à Fond-des-Blancs. Que de beaux souvenirs me viennent encore à la mémoire !

Dès le lendemain de mon arrivée, Sénat m'installait une balançoire dans un vieux magnolia, au fond de la cour, ou je passais beaucoup de temps. J'allais aussi rendre visite à mes oncles; et lorsqu'on passait devant le cimetière familial, Sénat savait que j'avais peur; pour me calmer, il me disait : « *mò yo se fanmi ou, yo pap fè ou anyen* – (ses morts sont tes ancêtres, ils ne te feront pas de mal). » Dans les sentiers difficiles, il prenait la bride de la « *bourrique* », et criait : « Paré (fais attention) ». Le soir, on se réunissait pour raconter des histoires et « tirer des contes ». Sénat m'avait fabriqué un petit instrument fait d'une boite de conserve, d'une ficelle et d'une branche d'arbres. Le bruit était supposé chasser les « *maringouins* » (moustique). Parfois, il nous chantait sa chanson favorite : la complainte d'un amoureux qui désirait avoir un petit peigne en écaille de caret, pour coiffer sa bien-aimée.

Une fois par semaine, nous allions a la rivière Dugué ou on profitait pour prendre un bon bain, laver le linge, faire boire les bêtes à volonté, et revenir avec des calebasses remplies d'eau. De retour à la maison, l'eau était utilisée avec parcimonie, et pour se laver, il fallait suivre une technique qui consistait à commencer, sans faute, par le visage. Nous allions aussi au marché et à la messe à Sainton. En ces occasions, Sénat mettait ses « *sapates* » (sandales). Un jour, assise sur la galerie, j'ai vue arriver Sénat de loin en titubant. J'ai dit à maman : « Sénat a bu » « Mais non, me répondit-elle, il est presqu'aveugle ! ». J'ai compris alors pourquoi il fonçait parfois sur un obstacle, et juste avant de le frapper tournait d'un coup sec !... J'ai commencé à le surveiller, à lui crier « *Paré* » (Fais attention) et souvent il me répondait « *m te wè l* » « J'avais vu. »

Je sais que je vais finir ma vie au Canada, mais lorsque viendra mon dernier souffle, il me semble que la traversée sera plus douce, si au bout du chemin, parmi tous les miens, je vois Sénat venir à ma rencontre et me dire : « *Mayou pitit mwen !* ». Une joie immense m'envahira, et je saurai alors que j'ai atteint le Paradis.

Marie-Elma Mitchell Duchesne
Tante Mayou

FINDING ERZILI

Gratitude is the heart's memory!

Thank you for

Giving
Defending
Reading
Writing
Cooking
Teaching
Learning
Working Damn Hard
Photographing
Speaking Out
Not Giving In
Evolving
Practicing
Painting
Trying
Waiting
Laughing Wildly
Walking with *Attitude*
Shining
Spanking
Hugging
Knowing
Pushing Back
Giving Back
Taking Back
Kissing
Scolding
Planting
Letting things go
Keeping me close
Modeling
Thinking
Nurturing
Creating
Crafting
Living
Every Moment

Love
Babette

My daughter

FINDING ERZILI

GLOSSARY

Ogou, is the Lwa of strength, courage and protection.

Agaou is the Lwa of thunder.

Erzili, also spelled **Èzili** is the Lwa of love.

Ginen is a spiritual and geographical place of our ancestors in Africa.

Teledyòl is the news by word of mouth.

A **Tito** is an elongated sweet chewy candy sold in the street of Port-au-Prince, Haiti.

Ayibobo, means "hail to".

A **Manbo,** is a female Vodou **healer**.

A **Hougan,** is a male Vodou healer.

Poul nan sòs, is chicken creole style.

Diri ak pwa, is rice and beans.

NGO, Non-Governmental Organization

FINDING ERZILI

OTHER WORKS BY THE AUTHOR

Armand, M. M. 2013. Healing in the Homeland-Haitian Vodou Tradition. Maryland: Lexington Books.

Armand, M. M. 2013. Haitian Vodou: Peace Begins Within – The Role of Religion in Peace Building, edited by T. Matyok, S. Byrne and J. Senehi. Maryland: Lexington Books.

Armand, M. M. 2009. "Poetry" In Brassage: An Anthology of Poems by Haïtian Women, edited by Michel, Toussaint, Roberson, 38–39. Florida: Multicultural Women Press. (Poems: Ogou, Ezili, Vodou Lakay Mwen)

Armand, M. M. 2009. Cultural Quarterly Magazine – Spring Issue 2004. (Poem: Dance)

Armand, M. M. 2007. "Taíno Enslavement and Resistance." In Encyclopedia of Slave Resistance and Rebellion, edited by J. Rodriguez, 498–503. Westport, CT: Greenwood Press.

Armand, M. M. 2006. "Marie Jeanne Lamartiniere." In Revolutionary Freedoms: A History of Strength, Survival and Imagination in Haïti, edited by C. Accilien, J. Adams, and E. Méléance, 85–90. Fort Lauderdale, FL: Caribbean Studies Press. (Poems: Ezili, Ogou)

Armand, M. M. 2004. "Conflict Resolution from Within." Conciliation Quarterly, 23(1): 13. (Poems: Bloodlines and Let Our Conscience Speak)

Armand, M. M. 2004. "Revolution Revolisyon Révolution." In Revolution, edited by Ella Turenne, 59. New York: Liv Lakay. (poem Revolution)

Armand, M. M. 2004. "Painting the Invisible: The Lwas of Haïtian Vodou." In The Descent of Lwas: The Journey through Haïtian Mythology. The Works of Hërsa Barjon, edited by Claudine Michel, 30. Broward County Library & California: The Center for Black Studies University.

Armand, M. M., (co-researcher) in T. K. Wah, eds. 2004. À la Recherche d'un Consensus Après 200 Ans d'Indépendence: La Structure du Système Social Haïtien & les Défis du Développement. New York: New Era Publishing.

Broward County Florida Public School System - Haitian Culture Curriculum K-5th and 6th-12th. 1998 per State of Florida Mandate.

Lutheran Ministries Haitian Curriculum for English For Speakers of Other Languages (ESOL) 1981

The poem entitled "Carrefour-Feuille" received the Nosside Mondial Poésie Award Honorable Mention in 2010.

PRASI (Practionner Research and Scholarship Institute) Scholar, 2003

KISKEYA PUBLISHING CO
www.kiskeyapublishingsco.com

FINDING ERZILI

FINDING ERZILI

MARGARET MITCHELL ARMAND

FINDING ERZILI

FINDING ERZILI
ISBN-13: 978 -1492992325
ISBN-10: 1492992321

Credits
Artwork, and Logo ©: Margaret Mitchell Armand
Vèvès Arts - Imani Collection by the author

FINDING ERZILI

Made in the USA
Charleston, SC
01 April 2014